MW01503210

# Music Makes My Day

Special thanks to these
great photographers:

Bud Fulginiti
Butch Worrell

Written by Heather Drockelman, Ed.D.
Designed by Courtney Brown

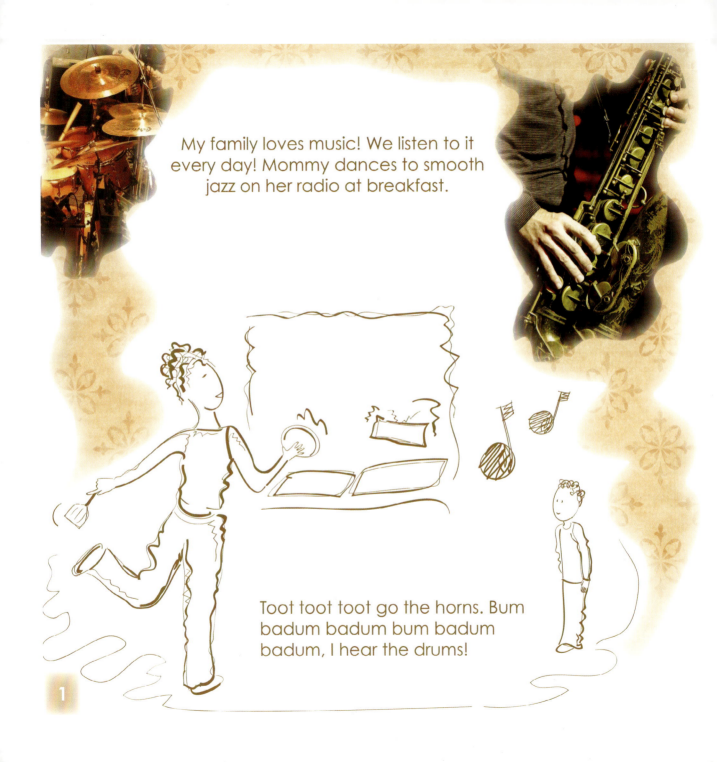

My family loves music! We listen to it every day! Mommy dances to smooth jazz on her radio at breakfast.

Toot toot toot go the horns. Bum badum badum bum badum badum, I hear the drums!

Daddy plays fun hip-hop music on the way to school every day. He slaps his knee to the beat of the drums.

Boom boom boom boom thump thump thump ba ba boom ba ba boom.

2

My teacher plays music when it's time to rest at school. The quiet music calms me down.

I listen closely to the sound of the violins and yawn. Yaaahh yaaahh yawwww nyyaahh yyawwww vvaaah vaaaah.

My mommy picks me up from school. She is listening to country music in her car.

Yee haw diddlee dee diddlee do! I listen to the guitar and the squeaky fiddle too.

4

Today Mommy and I stop for ice cream! There is fun rock 'n' roll music playing in the ice-cream shop.

Bop-bop-a-loo-bop a-womp-bam-boo! Shoowop shoobop! The sounds make my toes tap.

"Are you going to the parade today?" the ice-cream shop lady asks. "Can we, Mommy? Please?" I ask. Mommy and I jump in the car and race to the parade!

Vroom vroom vroom, the car engine makes music too!

"Do you hear that, Mommy? It sounds like a thousand drums!" I shout.

Rump-a-pum-pum boom-boom-bum! It looks like everyone in the parade has a drum!

There are so many different drums from all over the world! There must be drums everywhere!

Thump-thump-thump
bump-bump-bump
par-ump-a-pum-pum.

I see different instruments. They make sounds I have never ever heard!

Neer-neer-neer ba-na-neer-neer-neer-neer-neer-neer-neer-neer.

When I get home, I tell Daddy all about the parade and show him how the dancers moved.

At night, we remember the music we heard all day.

Then I remember that I get to hear my most favorite music of all – Mommy singing me good night!

La la la and good night, la la la la la la la, nee-nee-nah nee-nee-nah, mmmmmmm . . .